Patchwork Poetry ~ a vignette

Ananya Balike

BookLeaf
Publishing

India | USA | UK

Presentation by *BookLeaf Publishing*

Web: www.bookleafpub.com

E-mail: info@bookleafpub.com

ISBN: 9789357448376

First edition 2022

DEDICATION

To Hardik, who reminded me there was beauty in chaos. And (of course) to my loving and wonderful parents.

ACKNOWLEDGEMENT

First and foremost, I would like to sincerely
thank the people, who will remain unnamed
(there are 5), that inspired these poems. Without
them, these poems would not exist. As a result
of our interactions, I was able to learn and grow.
I was able to turn the remnants of broken glass
into a beautiful mosaic. I would also like to
thank BookLeaf Publishing for creating
#TheWriteAngle challenge and making this
poetry book possible.

PREFACE

Dear readers, it is my pleasure to introduce "Patchwork Poetry" to you. To elaborate on the reasoning behind the chosen title, "patchwork" refers to those quilts where small pieces of different cloth, varying in shape, size and colour, are sewn together to create the artwork. I have been meaning to publish these high school poems since 2018 now and it is almost surreal to see that actually happen. These poems were originally part of a longer poetry book I intended to publish, however the opportunity did not present itself, nor did I make the opportunity for myself (i.e. I kept procrastinating and stalling). I hand-selected these poems from a whole repertoire of 100+ poems. As the poems are varying in topic, sentiment, tone, and more, and are put together to create this particular artwork (the book); I came to conclude that "Patchwork Poetry" is by far, the most appropriate title to use. Although it may not seem as such, each of these poems were picked for a reason and instead of telling you directly what that is, I would like to invite the audience to interpret that for themselves. These poems are meant to represent only a particular time period of my life (high school). I hope that teenage angst is

something that others can relate well to.
Anyways, I'll keep this short and I hope you find
what you were looking for, reading this book.
Have a lovely read :)

That feeling

I went on a walk
After the rain stopped
I saw the snails outside,
And half of them have died.
Crushed into pieces,
Their home all gone
No longer protected
By the shell they have on
I imagined for a second
How that could have felt
If it were me;
I looked up at the sky,
And felt a giant's foot
Stepping on me

And for that brief moment,
That single tiny second,
I faded away into nothingness
Along with my shell I called home.
I merged with a painful vastness,
Desperate to find a way out of the loam.
My bones were crushed, my body was flattened,
And all this I felt, in that single (tiny) second

If a snail feels like this when its being stepped
on,
Why do I feel like this, even when no one is
stepping on me?
Why do I feel all this just by the thought of you?
That craving thought of us together, lost yet free.
A single spark, a memory of you, ignites my life
But also kills me inside
Because all you know is that you no longer want
me back,
But all I know, is that I can't forget the past

And these two simple facts combine to make a
rhyme,
To tell how it feels, when you're being crushed
into slime
I feel so helpless under this giant's foot,
A foot made of guilt and hurt unappealing
Be it a snail, or be it me,
We both feel the same, that same crushing
feeling.
Because I don't have a home, a shell to protect
myself from your harm
When all I can think of, is running carelessly
into your arms

The sound of my feet

It's all so quiet
That it feels incomplete
So silent you can hear
Only the sound of my feet

With all this calmness
I'm finally at peace
Gone are my woes,
Never felt this caprice

Nothing's in motion
Not even a summer breeze
It's all just so quiet;
I can hear myself breathe

With widened eyes I stare,
I can't escape fear's glare
My heart's pounding for a way out
My mind is filling up with doubt

But I turned this fear into glee,
A reason for me to put on a smile

Nature's voice calls out to me
The sound of home, undoubtedly

Although my breath does impede
It all just feels so unworried
As I marvel upon this breathtaking scene,
This sea of silence simply so serene

The neighbourhood's empty
As I walk down the street,
I can't hear anything
But the sound of my feet

lavender

from red to yellow to blue,
i'm stuck on this Lavender hue

reminiscing the times i used to have,
the light purple memories that come to my mind
as i yearn for the ungraspable past

i always sensed this day would come,
knowing Lavender like her, would be hard to
find
feeling a pain that will forever last

remembering it all,
with teary eyes' gloss
the dreams of blue that led to
this Lavender loss

just as she once told me, i believed she craved
constants
but she changed her favourite colour to pink
i didn't think much of it then, but… it all makes
sense
now i sit in this corner as i think and rethink

so many unanswered questions, my mind wishes
it knew
where did i go wrong? where and how did i
lack?
but i guess she's free to choose her favourite hue
who knows? maybe one day, her favourite
colour, will be black.

Unrequited love

Is it wrong to believe in fate?
Is it bad to think you could change?

Although this misery aches my heart,
And even though this silence keeps us apart
I still believe that things could change
I still believe that it's not too late

Let me make something clear,
You don't deserve my tears
But my heart skips a beat,
Every time you look at me

I was very happy with the trance I was in
But the magic's gone, and sadness was all I
found.
Now I dig my fingernails into my skin,
To find comfort whenever you're around

So that this pain could make me forget about the
hurt I feel from what you said,
So that physical pain is all I feel, but I feel this
agonizing one instead

All the lies you always said,

All the truth you never admitted,
All the pain, all the hurt;
The silent murder you committed.
This is more than injustice,
How can all your crimes be acquitted?
But what else can you really get
When your love is unrequited?

We used to be able to take on the world,
You made me feel like the luckiest girl.
But I guess you thought you had enough,
And now it's just unrequited love

With every word I
write

With every word I write
Drown out the sound of pain,
This hindering feeling
Of being lost in vain

With every word I write
You may think this a spiel,
But it's just the reality
Of how I truly feel

With every word I write
Take the pain away,
Make it seem alright,
Shun the hurt astray

With every word I write
Soak out the misery,
Let my worries wash away
And leave just the ecstasy

With every word I write

Consume the agony whole,
Mend my broken heart
And complete my shattered soul

With every word I write
Drain away the bad,
Dry my watery eyes
And take aside the sad

With every word I write
The unspoken story speaks,
Giving meaning to the tears
Absorbed by my cheeks

With every word I write
They tell the story no one knew,
About how every second of the day
I'm hopelessly in love with you

What once was mine

6 years old
Couldn't feel the cold
Frozen ice was all around her
But all she felt was how she was warmer
There was a time,
Where this was mine

7 years old
Oh, she was bold
She was carefree
And always happy
Couldn't care about the bad she faced
Wouldn't mind all the tests on her faith
There was a time,
Where this was mine

8 years old
Story untold
She was a dreamer, a visionary
She could take on the world, joyfully
She never quavered, and was oh, so happy
Wondering, and leaping, her thoughts were free

There was a time,
Where this was mine

15 years old
Moments uphold
Heartbreaks and misery
Lost all faith, trapped in agony
Dreams are shattered, and the heart in million
pieces
Every time there's a way out, her fear increases
Afraid to dream again, for the mere unwanted
feeling of being ripped apart and thrown away,
She has a heart, she has feelings, all she longs
for is to not fray

Yes, she's made mistakes
That lead to heartaches
But she's human, what's to be expected?
She's not a machine, she can't be perfected
We all know our flaws, our imperfections, what
we lack
But once glass is shattered, you can never bring
it back
Apologies and sorries, they were all conveyed
Broken hearts and stress and more stress, she's
dismayed

She feels the cold now, the dreaded, freezing,
bleak cold

She succumbs to it, without any warmth left to
hold
No more hope and no longer free
Tell me, how can this girl be happy?

I wish I could go back in time,
To bring back what once was mine

Held by yours

For whatever reason, you appeared in my
dreams
But for some reason, nothing's as it seems
I can't seem to get this thought out of me
I can't help feeling like we're meant to be

This feeling, powers me
Like a call from destiny

I can't let go from your soft embrace
Hand in hand, the world we'll face
Your fingers twining around mine,
Whispering everything's fine

Like waves gently caressing the sea shores,
My hand longs to be held by yours

Fairytale ending

A fairytale ending is too much to ask for
But all I want, is you, nothing more

A journey alongside you, is always worthwhile
Any day where you're there, is a day for a smile

Your love is a blindfold from which I can't get
away
Your love is a prison I can't seem to escape

You took away my breath and told me to breathe
You took away my words and told me to speak

I know it's not good to long for grandeur
And such happiness is too much to ask for,
But I still keep wishing and I still keep hoping
That one day, I'll get that fairytale ending

resonated

i was scrolling through instagram
and came across a post
the message echoed and haunted,
as if it were a ghost

the words reverberated, and resonated
as if a far away bell had been struck, but its rings
and vibrations still made their way to my ears

as if i was at the bottom of a well or at the edge
of a cave,
where my shouts were returned and hurled right
back

as if my tear drop had disrupted the stillness of
the lakes by causing their rippling

resonated.
fading, just like the waves that caress their
shores
the ones that get farther and farther, smaller and
smaller—fading.
fading away, and blindly blaming the distance
between

when it's not the distance and rather their
difference...any—
anyone could have seen,
the sea and the shore were meant to be
but, the sea and the shore, just couldn't be

resonated.
i don't remember her much anymore
i mean, i can still access the memories
but i can't feel them in the way i could before
and, it's part of the process i suppose…

i hope soon enough, they'll fade away
just like the waves
just like the moon that vanishes
once it's day

but never truly gone, even if it's no longer there
no longer visible, but still existing

resonated.
waves.
moon.

resonated.
no longer there.
but never truly gone.

resonated.

infinite.

Painted smiles

I stare down the creature looking back at me
Wondering how my reflection is not all I see
I see my eyes are filled with woe
Along with the hurt they do not show

So I take a paint brush and think a while
I look back at myself and draw on a smile
I might be hurt, but I won't let it show
Because that's one thing you don't deserve to know

My cheeks forced into a red of blushing shade,
To pretend that my insecurities can fade

But beneath all those painted smiles
I'm dying every day,
It's a shame you couldn't see
The hurt I tried to hide away

I draw on a lie, in the form of a big bright smile
So I can forget all the pain just for a little while

I know you no longer want me back
And unlike me, you're not stuck in the past

But no matter what, no matter it all
For you, I would still walk a thousand miles
And that's the heartbreaking truth,
The reason for my painted smiles

Childhood memories

A chest of childhood memories
Treasured more than gold
But I seem to have lost my keys
Over the days, growing old

Thorns

You were like a rose
A flower that I prose

So sweet and lovely to the eyes,
You made me believe all your lies
So calm and innocent,
Undeniably resplendent

But even a flower so pure and perfect,
So elegant with every aspect,
Has its imperfections that we can't miss
Rose: a serene beauty until that needle kiss

Because every rose comes with thorns
And even exuberance mourns
Happiness fading into sharp pain
Pricked, blood seeping from a vein

The petals sprouting its red mouth
The softness blooming out
Ending a seemingly long drouth
Quench my thirst of doubt

The flower blossoms and begs to speak
Just a moment, is all it seeks.

But my eyes, feeble, they seem to leak,
Droplets now soaking my cheeks

But I must stay strong, I can't reveal I'm weak,
Because the rose only wants havoc to wreak
Even such beauty comes with its price;
All my trust was sacrificed

The lies you've told,
The promises you never kept.
Your hands can't hold
The tears my eyes have wept.

I had put my faith in you,
That was my mistake
I didn't know your words weren't true,
That this rose was a fake

Too flawless, too perfect
Too good in every way
You were clearly too good to be true,
You're just a bad cliché

Although I believed you to be this flower,
You deprived the rose of its great power

You mocked the meaning of love,
And as if that wasn't enough,

You betrayed the meaning of rose with disdain; it scorns
Now when I see a rose, I'll always think of the thorns

I will dance

It's in my blood, coursing through my veins; the
desire to dance
Resonating in my ears, reverberating through my
body; this enticing trance

The applause awaits my every step,
And the audience holds their impeding breath -
In anticipation
The lingering silence in the air, as each
Awe-striking step marks my dedication and
Faithful passion

The world is my stage, I'll keep on dancing
Till my feet give out, and I can no longer hold
this stance
You can try to stop me, but I'll never stop,
I'll keep on dreaming to my heart's content; I
will dance

An ocean of lies

Hopelessly wanting to be untethered from his
reprise;
I grit my teeth, remembering his promises were
nothing but lies,
I pinch myself to try and break free from the
spell he's cast
But I'm enthralled and hypnotized by the
comfort of the past

His love is like a sumptuous repast
His eyes, they shine and are vast
His words are like a breath of spring or a
summer breeze
And I can't help but fall in love with the
memories

Every time a thought of him comes to my mind,
I'm reminded of the hurt he made me feel inside
And I'm trying so hard to leave the past behind,
But there's something about this pain I cannot
abide

I'm trying to move on,
I need these feelings gone
I'm trying in vain, that I know

But at least, I'm trying to let go

Even though every part of me tried and still
tries,
Every time I hear the word love, a little part of
me dies

Tear drops trickle down my cheeks,
Flooding my sight above,
But water that my eye leaks,
Creates an ocean of love

He beseeched forgiveness amidst,
A remorse filled look in his eyes
But all the things he says and does,
Creates an ocean of lies

No means no

No means no
It doesn't mean yes
It's not a secret language
Or a code you have to guess

It's not a hidden message that you have to
decode
It's a word with its exact definition; no

No means no
It doesn't translate to "yes, but I'm just playing
hard to get"
And do you know how long it took me to forget
About that night?
451 days and counting; but you don't care about
this fight

This battle I'm fighting everyday
Wondering how I could've changed that day
All the things I could've said, and could still say
But what's done is done, and that moment will
always stay

You might say it was a misunderstanding

Or that you thought I was hinting at you to keep
touching me
To keep making me feel uncomfortable—stop
pretending like you couldn't see it
Because you could.

You could see how I was fraught
And yet you just thought,
That you had this claim over my body?
When did you think you could even declare this
right?
When did I allow you to feel as if you had some
kind of hold over me?
My arms, my stomach, my limbs?
You had no right. And you knew it.
But that didn't matter to you, did it?

Did you not notice me shift every now and then
uneasily?
Did you not realize that I was avoiding, trying to
stay as far away from you as possible?
Can you seriously look me in the eye and tell me
that what you did, has a reason that is plausible?
Unbelievable.

I still get flashbacks, memories that haunt me
and taunt me
I still feel your hands grazing my skin,
Grabbing me in places even I've never been

"I know you like it",
Your words echo
I hear your voice, as it daunts me
You still don't know
What you've done,
You still don't realize all that you've caused

I bet you still think about that day as a conquest
A day where you had claim over a girl's chest

You invaded my space
When it wasn't your place

Then you had the audacity
After you violated my body
In 30 different ways
And you expected me to stay?

And every time I get reminded of this,
I just get ashamed and embarrassed
I get disgusted at myself and I feel at fault
Even though, NONE of it, was my fault
You created an unhealable wound, and you're
still pouring salt

Unforgettable, unchangeable,
You stole my innocence

Did you not hear me? Did you not see me
wince?
You chose to be deaf and blind, but
I've done worse; choosing to be mute
For so long, I've blamed myself. For so long,
I've tried to reason and dilute

Why did you do it?
Why didn't you think things through?
Because it's not just what you did,
But what you manage to still do

You may be gone, and out of my sight
But my mind just can't get rid of that night
My brain is clinging on to every detail, every
specifics
As if to search for anything I've done wrong;
Anything more I could've done to stop it

But I had said no, and I had said stop
So why the hell didn't you JUST FUCKING
STOP?
Did you ever take a moment to think about the
domino effect of feelings you've caused me to
have, when you stuck your hand inside my top?

No, because it doesn't matter.
NONE of this matters to you,

So why the fuck am I wasting my time, writing
all this about you?

After even months, I'm still not over it
And I know some have had it worse, but I'm
done keeping this a secret

I'm done pretending like it didn't bother me,
affect me;
Impact me in ways I can't begin to explain
Because the truth is, what you did, left a great
stain

When someone says no, they mean it, they mean
no
Not "yes", not "maybe". Our bodies are not for
show
When someone says no,
It means, "fuck off and leave me alone"
They're not being obscure or playing hard to get,
so don't.

Because "no", means "no".

Eight years old again

Abandoned thoughts of frivolous dreams
Being naive and youthful and oh, so carefree
Call it silly or stupid or dumb, but
Desperate to revisit this past, I'm

Eight years old again, joyful and free-spirited

If I were alone at the beach

If I were alone at the beach,
My first instinct would be to make you the sun
Basking in your essence,
As I crave your presence

As I watch the sunset and its vivid hues,
With its warmth and light that now suffuse
I'm looking straight ahead, over the waves of the
sea,
And you're one of the only things on my mind;
in me

If I were alone at the beach,
Perhaps you'd be more like the water
Spontaneity thriving, feeling adventurous,
Impulse pulsing and pulsating for us

As I revel in the waves that cradle me to sleep,
Holding me closely, making my heart leap
I sink in deep, beneath this liquid blanket, into
tomorrow

Run to your embrace; your body a bed, and your
shoulder a pillow

If I were alone at the beach,
Then maybe you'd best fit the description of
sand
You'd be every single grain around me,
The grains at my feet and the grains in my hand

Resting on top of you, wrapping me with your
warmth,
Sleeping in your arms, with the safeness you
bring forth
Not caring for the rain of doubt that had
previously stormed,
As I've learned to look straight ahead, to the
north

If I were alone at the beach,
Would you be better explained as a tree?
Providing me with shade and protection,
You'd be my shelter, my companion

You'd be stopping me from getting darker - in
all senses so to speak,
Cuddling up beside your roots, rendering me
meek
Reassuring me that things will be okay,
You'd be comforting me in every way

If I were alone at the beach,
Accordingly, maybe the sky is what you'd be
Indulging in its array of tints; taints of orange
and red
A coloration of sorts, a mosaic; a sky that has
bled

All I've known, until this moment, is the azure of
the day sky
The cerulean display, cloudless, delineating and
limning the extensive clarity
But at the sunset, at the dispersion of fiery
colours,
The interspersion of the blue amongst it all,
brings familiarity

If I were alone at the beach,
I think the evening breeze is what you'd be
(Because) I'd feel your presence everywhere,
Breathing you in longingly, as if you're elusive
and rare

Suffocating without your kisses, drowning
without respiration,
Intaking your intrinsic pull, needing you with
desperation
So there's your answer, darling, the one you've
beseeched,

The evening breeze is what you'd be, if I were
alone at the beach

A silent silhouette

A silent silhouette
Glistening from afar
A scintillating outline
Displaying the sea of stars

A serene serenade
By the summer breeze
A melodious rustling
From the leaves of trees

The susurrus of the stream
A surreal soliloquy
A sequestered scream
Of despondency

The stunning sunset
A spectacular view
Waves of regret
From ever loving you

This secluded scene
With a sad, soft scent
The slithering river seen
The swaying of grass, sent

The soothing voice of spring
The stillness of the silent night
Yet somehow the seagulls sing
Near the sandy shore's strayed sight

The silence seductive still
The nightingale sitting
Upon the window sill
As it starts its dulcet singing

Whispers of soothing voices
The darkness calling on
Summoning a dreary sonnet
Whilst its shadow lingers on

dear best friend,

i keep dreaming about you and when i awake,
the dream just fades
from my memory
and all i'm left with, is how i felt throughout the
projection
of my subconscious reality

every single time, it's the same—
the same strange nostalgic feeling
mixed in with a garnishing of guilt
i feel selfish for what i did, for giving up,
for abandoning the friendship we had built

but we both know the truth is
that you had left, without leaving,
long before i did

and although i feel selfish for chasing my own
happiness,
i feel foolish and stupid that i denied myself the
opportunity

i should've done what i did, months and months
ago

that way, i wouldn't have had to suffer the way
that i did—and still do
because no amount of verbal denying can hide
my heart's true feelings
i...
miss you.

i miss you and what we had—
and all the things we could have had
instead, i'm stuck shedding these tears
that you don't deserve

when i begged to salvage what we were,
your indifference thundered

of course i'm mad.
i am so infuriatingly angry.
how could you promise me so much and give so
less in return?
i admit, i wasn't perfect, but…
i hope at least i'd be enough

i hate that i still love you
when you so clearly don't
and i hate that i'll still keep thinking of you
when you so clearly won't

you stopped being my best friend long before i
stopped calling you that.

i hate myself for loving you
i hate myself for losing you
but more than anything…
i hate myself for still needing to write about you

Moments where I'm truly happy

• Running in an empty field that stretches far far away, that all you can see in the distance is the horizon; the blueness of the sky touching the greenness of the grass—the vastness of the meadow—I grin

• Lying on top of the monkey bars of an abandoned park, staring blankly at the sky and examining the intricate shapes of the clouds I remark

• Walking on a path at night, scared to death of stepping on snails or of frogs leaping out...yet walking bravely, with my head held high—and letting out a shriek because I mistook a moth to be a frog—then out of relief, out comes a sigh

• Experiencing a waterfall; where the waterfall claims me as its own, the wind hitting my face and the water gushing, surpassing my feet—the truest of truest smiles forms and takes over me,

because even in this hurricane, I still feel the
peace

• Dancing to my heart's content; when I finally
let go—I start to dance systematically, but as the
time progresses, the beat takes control and
moves my body for me—eventually, I've lost all
control and my body moves on its own; I've let
go… no longer able to stop my rapturous
laughter, as if that's all I've ever known

• When I'm with you; no, I don't mean
physically with you, but in my mind with
you—when I reminisce our moments and
cherish our memories; think about what's
happened and what's yet to happen—when I'm
in my mind, with you...I feel truly at peace

Do you hear that

Do you hear that?
That is the sound of silence.
That is the sound of unspoken thoughts.
The sound of words never said aloud.
A hymn to all the stories never told, all the
secrets lingering in the air.
It is the moment right after a gasp, a moment
when all you can hear - is nothing, yet
everything.
Because if you listen carefully, silence isn't
quiet. It's the thoughts being whispered from
mind to mind, a path being paved, a maze being
made, the blues and purples radiating and a deep
breath of green. Red and pink circulating, orange
and brown striking. But most of all, silence is
the grey emptiness. The moment where you
await for the sun to rise, or for the sun to set; the
brief second where everything is grey, in
anticipation of all the colours yet to burst.
Silence isn't about the tranquility. Silence is
about the fragility. Silence is when you can hear
every single raindrop hitting the ground, and
hear the pitter patter sound upon your window.
Silence is when you can hear just the clouds
moving, across the azure sky, when you walk

down the path, and it's just you and your strides. The sound of your feet, crunching the leaves as you walk by. Silence is the moment right after a lion's roar, and right before a cricket's chirp. When you can hear the batting of the wings of any bird set to soar, and hear the sound of snow falling upon your nose. That's silence. When you can feel an ant crawl on your hand and perceive it as just that - an ant crawling on your hand. That's silence. When you can smell the burnt wood and taste the crispness of the fallen leaves without even touching it. That's silence. When you run your fingers across the bark, appreciate its rigidness and accept it for the way it is. That's silence. When you can see the spring blooms, the flowers that blossom, light pink; when you can hear the sea shore, and taste the salt of the ocean by simply listening to it. When you can smell the heat of the sun, and feel yourself sinking in the sand beneath your bare feet. When you hear the singing of birds, the greeting of chickadees, and the ribbits of frogs. That's silence. When you can feel the vibrations of the waterfall, hear the babbling of the streams, catch the whispering of the waves; when you can hear nothing and everything, that's silence.